Finders

Secrets of Success

Finders

Secrets of Success

by

T. D. Bunce

River of Gold Publishing

Finders: Secrets of Success

First paperback edition published in the United States of America, 2015

ISBN-10: 0-9963819-0-2   ISBN-13: 978-0-9963819-0-1

10   9   8   7   6   5   4   3   2   1

For permission requests ro reproduce selections from this book, write to the publisher, subject line: Attention: Permissions Coordinator, at tdbunce366@gmail.com.

Colophon: This book is set in Garamond, Garamond Bold, Garamond Italic, Garamond Bold Italic. The text is set, 14/16.8 x 27.

www.Riverofgold.com

Table of Contents

Introduction

In the past three years I have spoken with dozens of metal detectorists at shows, club meetings, sponsored hunts, or in the field. My experience to date is that year after year 10% of detectorists find 90% of the treasure. I set myself the challenge of trying to determine why these people were so consistently successful?

This book will introduce you to some of the most successful metal detectorists in North America. They share their critical success factors that have led them to discover objects of value year after year. By reading this informative and entertaining collection of profiles of successful detectorists, I believe you will understand more about the hobby, possibly give it a try, and at the very least have a higher probability of success if you do.

T. D. Bunce
2015

"It is the responsibility of every individual who pursues this hobby to fully understand that their behavior in the field represents us all."
— Anonymous

Acknowledgments

My heartfelt thanks to all the Metal Detector Club Presidents across North American who provided the names of those showcased in this book.

Additionally, a special thanks to George Streeter whose advice and guidance throughout the formation and development of this book allowed me to take my vision to reality.

Thank you to my family and friends who believed I could do it.

A final thank you to Jenna Brook and Yvette Grimes who provided the technical guidance to publish this book.

T. D. Bunce
2015

CHAPTER 1
Altamont Legend
Bob Lavoy

The community of Altamont (a small village in the town of Guilderland), New York, has approximately 1,700 residents, and is located south of Schenectady and west of Albany. It lies at the crossroads of major east/west and north/south highways near the Helderberg Mountains. The tree-lined downtown area is filled with specialty shops, restaurants, and services.

The Susquehanna Railroad passed through Altamont from 1863 to 1963, bringing passengers to the gateway of the Adirondack Mountains. Rich in history, the area was a known pathway for early settlers and First Nations people who hunted, fished, and trapped in what is now known as the 50,000 acre Adirondack Preserve.

Successful metal detectorist Bob Lavoy is well known to the Altamont community. Bob has been metal detecting since 1960, and in that time has discovered fourteen sunken ships in Lake George dating from 1758. His discoveries have resulted in raising a substantial number of artifacts. This early success locked him into a lifetime passion for treasure hunting..

The introduction of metal detectors in the 1970's caught his curiosity. As a result metal detecting became his livelihood. Armed with these new instruments Bob focused his efforts in the French and Indian War, and Revolutionary War encampments. His research paid off enabling him to recover a vast collection of regimental buttons, trade axes, belt axes, cannonballs, and musketry.

The lure of sunken ships that had started his treasure hunting career, eventually brought Bob to Florida waters and the potential riches they held. Armed with historic maps of the waters surrounding Florida, and knowledge he had gained studying hurricane patterns from the 1700s, Bob once again found success. Pieces of eight, doubloons, gold coins, jewelry, and artifacts added to the Lavoy Collection.

Bob continues to be an avid treasure hunter, business owner (North East Metal Detector), and President of the Empire State Metal Detecting Association. He still *mines* the beaches of Florida, and the Caribbean, and can be seen wearing some of his found bounty.

Bob has discovered a new path for marketing his artifacts – eBay. Hand forged tools from the 1700s and 1800s appear to have a ready audience of collectors with a thirst for owning a piece of history.

Bob still finds the time to accept every opportunity to speak at schools on the subject of metal detecting and its role in discovering and preserving history.

Last but far from least, Bob has developed a program called "Extending Life Metal Detecting." The course is directed primarily at senior citizens to get them off the couch, into the fresh air, and enjoying the benefits and camaraderie of the hobby.

Critical Success Factors

- Use the local library and Internet to understand the history of the area where you live. Copy old town maps that may show the location of the original homes which might now be empty lots or foundations.
- Learn your detector, learn your detector, and learn your detector. Shop owners, YouTube.com, manufacturer's websites, detector manuals, and

DVDs can provide you with a wealth of knowledge about the detector you own.

- Knock on doors when you see a property that looks promising. Offer to look for specific items the landowner may have lost.

- Take your metal detector on vacation. An early walk on the beach or park provides exercise and the potential for finding items of value.

CHAPTER 2

The Grand Lady
of Metal Detecting
Rosemary Sanders

Pensacola, Florida, is the home of the Pensacola Historical & Treasure Hunting Association, and Rosemary Sanders, the "Grand Lady of Metal Detecting."

Pensacola is the westernmost city in the Florida Panhandle. Situated on Pensacola Bay, the city proper contains approximately 50,000 residents, and another 450,000 in the surrounding area. One of the area's most famous attractions is the United States Naval Station, home of the Blue Angels demonstration team.

The earliest recorded inhabitants were referred to as the Muskogean speaking people, or as the Spanish named them, the Pensacola. In 1559 the Spanish arrived and established the first settlement. The area changed hands several times from Spain to France, and then to the English in 1763, and back to Spain in 1781 after the Battle of Pensacola.

Andrew Jackson became the first provisional governor in 1821 when Florida was annexed to the colonies. The United States purchased Florida from Spain in 1891 for $5 million as part of the Adams-Onis Treaty.

Because Pensacola is rich in history from the time of Muskogean speaking tribes, to the occupations by the Spanish, French, English, and American colonies, it is a metal detectorist's dream. Adding to the rich history, the Florida Panhandle has been in the path of hurricanes for centuries. In the past 40 years over ten hurricanes have either directly hit or glanced by the area. The result of these attacks by Mother Nature, and the resulting shifting sands from storm surges, have provided the metal detecting community continued opportunity for discovering artifacts.

Rosemary Sanders has been a fixture in the metal detecting community for the past 36 years. She started with a

Whites Classic I in 1970, and soon became hooked on metal detecting. A year later, she upgraded to a Whites 5000, and then a year after that she purchased a Whites 6000. By now metal detecting and the quest for historic relics had become her passion. In 1990 she opened up a Metal Detecting store carrying all the major brands of detectors and accessories, providing a one stop shopping experience for the Florida Panhandle.

In the early 1990s she founded the Pensacola Historical & Treasure Hunting Association, where she has been President for the last 24 years. She was the host of the Jasco Treasure Show for five years. It was a one-hour live program on local Channel 6 station BlabTV.

Despite major heart, hip, rotator cuff, neck fusion, and hip surgery, Rosemary continues to metal detect at least once every week throughout the year. Doctor's orders, following several surgeries, to slow down have fallen on deaf ears. She has even been known to metal detect from her walker.

Currently, Rosemary uses two primary metal detectors: a Fisher CZ20 in the water (yes, she routinely wades up to her waist in the Gulf), and a White's MXT on dry land. Her basic belief is to work with one detector at a time until it becomes part of you.

In 2000, Rosemary and John Sanders (her former husband) were inducted into the Treasure Hunters Hall of Fame, an honor reserved for only the best of the best who have made personal, if not professional, contributions to the metal detecting world. George Streeter, the founder and director of the Hall of Fame, speaks very highly of Rosemary's long-term dedication to the hobby. "Her persistent feedback toward improving equipment, or standing up to those who would block our rights to detect, are worthy of praise."

A few of the noteworthy relics Rosemary has discovered over the years:

- Union sword belt plate
- Confederate States of America belt plate
- Spanish gold cob
- 1800's pocket watch (in working order)
- Large collection of musket and Minié balls
- Two 10" 80 lb. cannon balls
- 150 axe heads
- A button collection covering 200 years of American history

Although relics are her preferred treasure of choice, she has accumulated a significant collection of coins, rings, and other jewelry. Among her finds are several dozen coins from the mid-1700's to mid-1800's, a diamond and sapphire necklace, and several display cases of gold, silver, and diamond rings.

Critical Success Factors

- Find a metal detector you are comfortable with and stick with it. Competence is not to be confused with technology. The detector is a tool that is only as good as the person holding it.
- Take every opportunity to defend our hobby. Don't leave it to someone else to do it for you. Opportunities to attend town, regional, or state meetings where

our rights to detect are being challenge, needs us all present to defend them.

- Detecting beaches at night often produces the most valuable finds. For safety's sake always "buddy up" when hunting after dark. The lack of crowds at night, and the noise disruptions of the day, often increases your ability to focus on hearing that faint sound leading to a major find.

CHAPTER 3
Lawman
Steve Baldwin

After 23 years in law enforcement investigating crimes, and practicing law for the State of New Hampshire, Chief Steve Baldwin has applied the same skill set to metal detecting. To be successful in either environment requires patience and meticulous attention to detail.

According to Chief Baldwin, processing a crime scene and approaching a site to metal detect are very similar. Walking into a crime scene the lead investigator is required to gather physical evidence and create an image as to what may have occurred. Moving this ability to the field requires analyzing a site and visualizing where major and minor traffic patterns may have occurred. Often a landmark will assist in creating a vision and a metal detecting strategy. A 200-year-old tree where people may have stopped to rest and seek shade on a hot summer's day, or a stone wall where people may have walked the boundaries of the property, or a remote gate in a pasture, are all things to take into consideration. Most metal detectorists head for the front walkway, mailbox, or paths to outbuildings. Steve tends to leave these areas behind and search the corners of the property where workers may have led oxen, draft horses, or driven tractors on a daily basis, planting, harvesting, or tending livestock.

Patience and perseverance are the most necessary ingredients for a successful trip afield. The step most amateurs skip in their rush of enthusiasm to be on a potential site is to fully understand their equipment. Manufacturers' websites, DVDs, metal detecting forums, treasure magazines, and regional retailers provide a wealth of information and guidance to those new to the hobby.

Taking the time to create a test garden and trying various equipment settings before you arrive onsite will increase your productive time, and success. Steve points to the ease with which human nature blames the equipment when expectations aren't met. Accepting that it's you who is not working, as opposed to blaming the equipment, is the first step to actually becoming proficient. Once you have moved beyond blame and started developing the right attitude and patience, you'll find a whole new enjoyable experience.

Some tricks of the trade that have helped Steve amass his collection of coins, artifacts, and fine jewelry, center on his intentionally distancing himself from the crowds. Whether it's at the beach, in a cornfield, or at an historic site, you will often find him a substantial distance away. This behavior is not intended to be antisocial, but has been one of the factors resulting in him recovering many of his most valuable finds. While others speed hunt, that is metal detect at the pace of a rabbit, Steve marks out a smaller area and thoroughly, slowly, and patiently searches it. This again is where his background in law enforcement has served him well. Crime scene evidence recovery requires significant patience and the skill to know what to look for. Steve carries a number of colored tent stakes to define the area he is detected. He will thoroughly cover that defined area before moving the stakes forward. This slow, methodical approach often results in picking up that faint signal that might be missed by the rabbits.

Examples of Steve's patience, perseverance, and astounding success:

- .925ct Silver ring with a .50ct amethyst stone
- 14ct Women's twin heart symbol of love ring
- 18ct Women's love knot wedding band

- 18ct Women's gold cocktail ring, surrounded by 10 diamonds and a 2.5ct emerald aquamarine stone

- 14ct Women's evening ring with a .5ct marquise cut garnet stone

- 14ct Women's designer crafted 7.5ct precious stone in an Art Deco bracelet

Critical Success Factors

- Learn and fully understand your equipment. Don't blame it for not finding and recovering valuable targets.

- Slow down and really listen to what your detector is trying to tell you. Covering as much ground as possible is not an effective method for achieving success.

- Visualize what and where various activities might have occurred before starting to detect a site. Look for landmarks that might provide valuable clues where you should begin detecting. Move away from the obvious and focus your efforts on the hidden.

CHAPTER 4
Corporal Gillespie
Darwin Gillespie

For the past 27 years, Darwin Gillespie of Port Byron, Illinois, has been a member of a Civil War Reenactment Group – the 8th Kansas Calvary Volunteer Infantry Company H. His passion for Civil War artifacts has taken him on a journey of discovery across 11 states (Illinois, Iowa, Missouri, Virginia, West Virginia, South Carolina, Kentucky, Colorado, Michigan, Wisconsin, Ohio), and the United Kingdom. Approximately 14 years ago, Darwin purchased his first metal detector, a Bounty Hunter Sharp Shooter II, and began searching for artifacts and silver coins.

In his quest for Civil War artifacts, Darwin has worked in cooperation with Museums, Historical Societies, and State Archeological Teams. By adapting a method of mapping an area to be detected and flagging the site of a target recovery, he has gained the respect and cooperation of these organizations.

Port Byron is a short distance from the Illinois Quad City area. This area, directly on the Mississippi River, is rich in history associated with the Civil War, our nation's early westward expansion, and of course all that goes with riverboat travel. Property in proximity to old forts, supply depots, and troop encampments has contributed to his personal collection, as well as that of the organizations with which he has joined forces.

Artifacts are not the only focus of Darwin's metal detecting. In 2014 he recovered a total of 284 silver coins.

To identify areas of high target potential Darwin employs the use of the earliest aerial or plat maps he can find in a rather unique way. He compares these maps year after year to discover where parks, ball fields, fairgrounds, or schoolyards have move or shifted locations. By studying this information and then overlaying a Google earth map, he is able to pinpoint areas of detecting interest. Once on a site he makes the most of his time by searching very methodically in one direction then turning to search across the area in a diagonal direction. In some cases, if the area has a large amount of trash, he will change to a smaller coil and repeat the entire process. In one park, known to be heavily hunted, he recovered over 50 silver coins using this method. To focus on silver coins, Darwin only responds to a coin signal deeper than six inches. Although it can be said that he could potentially leave a number of silver coins behind, his success speaks for itself.

Small sampling of Darwin's success in the field:

- Civil War Union Eagle breast plate
- Collection of Minié balls, round balls, and cleaner rounds
- Confederate private's wax seal stamp
- Confederate staff officer's uniform button
- Bronze Age axe (1500-1400 BC)
- Coins dating to the Roman Empire
- 1877 CC seated Liberty dime

Critical Success Factors

- In the search for artifacts, take the time required to find historical locations. Historical Societies are an excellent source of information leading to a successful hunt. Join or work with these organizations and demonstrate to them how cooperation can serve both the organization and the detectorist.

- There are no shortcuts to consistent metal detecting success. It requires research, talking to knowledgeable individuals in the area, and applying good old fashion problem solving skills to determine where high value areas might be located.

- Having a metal detecting business card can make the difference between a yes or no to detect on private property. But, don't just hand the owner a card and believe that's all that's required. Engage the owner in a conversation about the history of his/her property and compare it to your own research. After a successful hunt, it is highly recommended that you purchase a gift card at a local restaurant and give it to the landowner.

- If you are serious about this hobby, and are committed to the long haul, purchase the best equipment you can afford. Having equipment that can differentiate, discriminate, and provide good depth detection will pay for itself many times over.

CHAPTER 5
Coin Man
John Leiker

Kansas City, Kansas, is situated at the confluence of the Kansas and Missouri Rivers. The first thing that comes to mind when Kansas City comes up is the famous Kansas City Steak, or Kansas City Style Barbeque. But Kansas City is much more than that, boasting a rich American heritage.

Originally the area drew trappers, scouts, and traders harvesting the rich abundance of furs from the nearby forests and waters. Early settlers on their way west passed through Kansas City, picking up the Santa Fe or the Oregon Trails. The Lewis and Clark expedition passed through in 1804, camping on what is now referred to as Kaw Point where the Kansas and Missouri Rivers join. In 1863, the Missouri/Kansas border was the site of one of the first Civil War battles. In 1871 Kansas City went on to become one of the major cattle drive destinations, and remained so until the floods of 1951. Today Kansas City has become a modern metropolitan city embracing its history and forging a future with investments in excess of $6 billion to revitalize the downtown area.

The scores of early settlers passing through, and those who choose to stay, created fertile ground for the modern metal detectorist.

John Leiker has been metal detecting the trails, parks, and original school sites in the Kansas City area for 44 years. Known by his Club members as the "Coin Man," John has recovered over 12,000 coins in the last three years alone.

John remarked, "I never kept track of the numbers of coins until my fellow detectorists hung the name on me."

In 2012, John started to keep count, with his peak year being just over 5000 coins recovered. He claims not to have a formal exercise program to keep fit, but finding and recovering 3,000-5,000 coins per year requires a significant amount of bending and digging that obviously qualifies. The number of coins he potentially recovered over the course of 44 years detecting is staggering.

Although John's focus and passion has been coins, he volunteers his metal detecting expertise to local law enforcement, as well as responding to lost and found requests in the local newspaper.

One of his key sources for finding sites to detect on is the word of mouth shared at garage sales. John travels older neighbors around Kansas City on the weekends looking for both advertised and non-advertised garage sales.

John has noted, "Spending a few dollars here of there and striking up a conversation with the older folks on site has paid dividends time and time again."

Examples of John's Success as the Coin Man:

- Quantity – 12,000+ coins recovered since 2012
- Quantity – 228 coins found in a single day (Best Day)
- Ten silver dimes
- One silver quarter
- One silver half dollar
- Two silver dollars (1923 & 1935)
- Fifty-Four coins found in a local park in a single day
- One silver nickel
- One silver dime
- Two gold rings (10ct and 14ct)

Critical Success Factors

- Visit the local public library(ies) and search historical archives specific to original schoolhouses. The original site may now be a housing development or retail mall, but often the surrounding areas can produce valuable finds.

- Study early tax maps to determine the location of the earliest homes, parks, and public gathering areas.

- Take the time each week to review garage sale notices advertised in the local newspaper, Craigslist, or tacked onto trees and poles. Make a list of those that appear to be in older neighborhoods, and make a point of stopping and talking to the landowners.

CHAPTER 6
Combat Metal Detector
Jason Sevene

How in the world can the words combat and metal detecting link together? Very simple, the training the 82nd Airborne Division of the U.S. Army provided New Hampshire's Jason Sevene has paid off time and time again. The value of deep reconnaissance, living in the wild, and keeping a positive attitude are characteristics of a well-trained soldier.

Jason has applied his soldier's experience and training to metal detecting and the pursuit of finding "treasure" year-after-year. At the first signs of winter releasing its frozen grip, Jason heads to out-of-the-way sites to detect. His feeling is that if a site is not a challenge to reach then it has probably been hunted before. Furthermore, if need be he prepares to stay on a target site for several days in order to thoroughly cover the area.

Jason's current occupation as a railroad conductor plays a significant role in finding high probability locations that others may not see. Train routes through both urban and rural areas often provide leads on which he can follow up. These sites are not necessarily remote in nature, but possibly relate to historical events, or early gathering areas. Old railroad station locations, old railroad beds, and repair depots are all on his deep research list.

The success that Jason has had is substantial. Samplings of his historic coin finds are:

- 1723 Woods Hibernia halfpenny
- 1730 King George II halfpenny
- 1816 Matron head cent
- 1794 Liberty Cap large cent
- 1853 Half dime

- 1837 Capped Bust half dollar

Coins appear to be the focus of Jason's metal detecting, but he has also recovered antique pistols, buckles, buttons, and commemorative plates, as well as several pieces of exquisite jewelry.

Critical Success Factors

- A positive "never give up" attitude and patience are a must, despite weather conditions or travel distances, or the ever present challenge of gaining permission to metal detect on private lands.

- Complete familiarity with your equipment is a must. Buy the best you can afford and then be willing to put the hours in to fully understand your equipment's positive and negative characteristics. Blaming the detector for lack of finds is not an acceptable excuse.

- Finding a metal detecting mentor is not an easy task. Try to find a mentor who will make certain you are on the right track in terms of technique, equipment, and site selection.

- Spending time researching prospective areas to metal detect increases your odds of finding something of value tenfold. The odds of stumbling onto a highly productive area are not in your favor. Do your homework first.

- Physical conditioning is often overlooked as most people consider metal detecting to be a hobby, as opposed to a sport requiring physical conditioning. The better shape you are in the more effective and longer you can stay focused in the field.

CHAPTER 7
Speaker-Treasure Seeker Michael Warren

ichael is an Executive Sales Management Consultant providing sales leadership to medical and technology companies. Residing in history rich New England, he has leveraged his love for history with a newly found hobby: metal detecting. Michael has been detecting for just over two years. His approach to detecting is to apply the same attention to details and planning that his career demands. His adventures have resulted in once-in-a-lifetime finds, and have created many opportunities to share engaging stories. Getting involved with speaking to Museums, Historical Societies, Rotary Clubs, and students about the history of New England and his finds related to the period, has built a base of supporters. It is not uncommon for Michael to leave a speaking engagement with several leads, or even direct permission to detect private lands. In an effort to find and network with others who share the same passion for history and metal detecting, he and his son joined a local metal detecting club. Soon he became a regular winner of "Finds of the Month" in the categories of coins and artifacts. His passion for promoting an ethical approach to metal detecting, coupled with finds related to the early settlement of New England, led to his being elected to the club's Executive Committee in 2015. Club members now look forward to and anticipate his sharing his latest finds.

A sample of the finds Michael has recovered and shared with others over the past two years:

- 1787 Fugio cent – Excellent condition issued two years before George Washington was elected President

- Two 18th Century Spanish silver coins – a pistareen and a 1 real

- Over sixty 18th and 19th century buttons

- 1735 King George II halfpenny

- Two Phoenix Buttons – 4th and 30th regiment

- State Coppers from Massachusetts, Connecticut, and New Jersey

- 1858 Flying Eagle cent

- Indian Head pennies – 1864, 1865, and 1869 – found together

Critical Success Factors

- Seek opportunities to share your enthusiasm for the metal detecting hobby with organizations and individuals who share an interest in recovering and preserving history.

- Use your local library's history section to discover the origin and location of high potential sites.

- Obtain U.S., State, and local historical maps, then overlay current maps to pinpoint sites of interest. The Library of Congress website (www.loc.gov) has a huge map collection of the United States, and the world, available for free download. Most of the maps are in extremely high resolution.

- Design a "metal detecting" specific business card (or, ask a friend to help). This gives landowners your contact information, and shows a level of professionalism that goes a long way toward being granted permission to metal detect their property.

- Avoid the word "hunt" when addressing a landowner, as it might bring up a negative image of your intentions. The words "metal detect" are more descriptive and positive.

CHAPTER 8
Show Me
Mike Moutray

Missouri is known as the "Show Me" state. Representing the state's motto and that of his personal values is Mike Moutray from St Louis, Missouri. Mike has been a member of the Midwest Coin Shooters and Historical Club of St. Louis, for a number of years. In the past he has served as Hunt Master, Club Librarian, and member of the Research Committee.

In recent years, Mike has focused his efforts on promoting and educating (show me) newer detectorists on the proper method of retrieving a target.

Mike advises, "Learning how to recover a target without leaving *any* trace is critical, not only for the enjoyment of our hobby, but as the single most important factor to gain permission to detect sites that would be otherwise closed to detecting."

St. Louis has been well known throughout the 19th, 20th, and 21st centuries as a major port on the Mississippi River, and gateway to westward expansion. Lewis and Clark began the epic journey of their Corps of Discovery starting from St. Louis in 1804, and returning in 1806, having traveled to the Pacific shores and back.

Riverboats and steamships carrying goods and passengers back and forth between St. Louis and New Orleans led to its early expansion and colorful history. Today the famous Gateway Arch welcoming visitors by auto, truck, or airplane symbolizes its historic roots as the Gateway to the West.

Gateway to the West, historic river port, and crossroads of famous travelers, the St. Louis area offers the modern metal detectorist many choices of what and where to detect.

One of the most attractive areas to metal detect, is Forest Park in the center of the city. Covering nearly 1300 acres (larger than New York's Central Park), and having been the site of the 1904 World's Fair, it has the potential to provide some very interesting finds. An estimated 12 million visitors a year pass through the park enjoying its natural beauty, the Zoo, Art Museum, Museum of History, and Museum of Science. This is one of Mike's favorite areas to detect. He has shared his knowledge of Forest Park's history, and productive areas to detect. He has exhibited many artifacts found there to the Club.

Mike has 33 years of metal detecting experience not only in his native St Louis, but also across 15 states, resulting in an amazing collection of coins and historic artifacts.

Examples of Mike's consistent success:

- Seven Spanish reales (including a 1800 eight real)

- 1916 Standing Liberty quarter

- Thirty-two Morgan silver dollars

- 1909 SVDB Wheat penny/1909S Wheat penny/ 1914 D Wheat penny

- Twenty – Two-cent pieces

- Two – Twenty-cent pieces

- Hundreds of seated silver coins

Critical Success Factors

- Pick a State you are interested in detecting. Use the Internet to make a list of every county in the state, then record all the historical sites, courtyards, or points of interest, by city and town. Prioritize the list in relation to the age of the site. Use old maps or satellite images to refine the search area.

- Old courtyards are often productive. Check in with the local police or sheriff's office to determine if metal detecting is permitted on the property.

- Whenever possible, spend time in the local library to review historical archives and property maps. The librarian may know someone who has significant local knowledge not found in written records.

- Represent our hobby positively through consciously retrieving targets without leaving a trace or damaging an area.

CHAPTER 9
Maine Builder Abe Harrington

Topsham, Maine, population less than 10,000, lays 26 miles north of Portland, and is less than five minutes from Brunswick. The town is most noted for the Topsham Fair, celebrating 161 years of continuous operation in 2015.

The Abenaki First Nation people were the first known inhabitants of the area, where they camped, hunted, and fished along the banks of the Androscoggin River. English settlers named the town of Topsham after Topsham, England in the early 1700s, and it soon became a fast growing center of development. Lumber, Tanneries, and Feldspar mills were scattered along the Androscoggin River, along with a pocket watch, nail, and shingle factories in the town. Brunswick and Topsham were also considered to be an integral link of the Underground Railroad which passed through 14 states, providing an escape route to Canada.

Abe Harrington, a resident of Topsham, is a well-regarded home builder, who only recently embraced metal detecting as a hobby. Prior to purchasing his first detector, he was a long time student of Colonial history. Abe spent hour after hour immersing himself in every document he could find relative to early activity along the mid-Maine coastal area. Starting out with an in-depth knowledge of the area, its early history, and his many contacts developed through his business, Abe was destined to be successful at metal detecting. With only two years detecting experience behind him, his finds are impressive.

Examples of Abe's success:

- 1652 Pine Tree shilling
- 1664 Potosi mint cob

- 1760 Irish Hibernia halfpenny

- 1772 Half real

- 1782 Spanish silver – Carolus III

Critical Success Factors

- Be prepared and equipped to pursue a documented fragment of information, or even a hunch, as to the location of a Colonial site. Paddle, hike, or cross swamps if necessary in pursuit of a targeted site.

- Do not get discouraged if after a long day reaching a potential site, it turns out not to produce anything of value or interest. When a field trip does produce, all of the empty trips are forgotten.

- Dig every signal above iron. The effort will often produce the most valued finds at the end of the day.

- Commit to each site visited as if you will never return. Make the effort to stay all day and go over each area until you are convinced that you have covered it sufficiently – then go over it again.

- If you are fortunate to have a business that puts you in touch with homeowners, suppliers, and sub-contractors, tell them about your hobby. Word travels fast, particularly in small communities, and can produce some amazing results.

CHAPTER 10
Public Works
Bill Stowers

Boston, Massachusetts, with a population of 650,000, is the 24th largest city in the United States. On a grander scale, taking in what is known as Greater Boston, the number swells to 4.5 million. Founded in 1630, Boston is also one of the oldest cities in the United States. The roots of our democracy are part of its history and our heritage.

Today Boston is a modern city, recognized as a center of technological innovation, education, medicine, and culture. The Massachusetts Institute of Technology, Harvard University, Tufts University, Brandeis University, and the University of Massachusetts, are a small sample of the quantity and quality of higher education offered in the greater-Boston area. Massachusetts General Hospital, Brigham & Women's Hospital, Children's Hospital, the Dana-Farber Cancer Institute, New England Baptist Hospital, and the Massachusetts Eye & Ear Infirmary are world-renowned centers of medical excellence. Boston ranks third in the country in its commitment to establishing and preserving land for parks and family recreation.

The greater Boston Area has a substantial seacoast on the Atlantic Ocean, with many beaches, both public and private. Revere Beach, Cranes Beach, and Carson Beach are easily accessible to Boston residents and visitors.

Nearly 400 years of history, a large and diverse population, acres of parklands, and easy access to the ocean makes the Greater Boston area a mecca for metal detecting.

Bill Stowers has been detecting these parks and beaches for over 30 years. He is currently retired from the Department of Public Works. As an active employee, he had the opportunity to become very familiar with city-owned parks and beaches open to detecting.

Studying the early DPW maps and their relationships to older neighborhoods, and studying history books specific to neighborhood development, has paid off over and over. In addition, daily walks along the beach with and without a detector, observing the tides in various seasons and various times of day, provided Bill with an advantage finding where the "sweet spots" were likely to be. In recent years Bill has expanded his research to the United Kingdom, joining group expeditions in search of coins and artifacts from the days of knights and kingdoms.

Here's a small sampling of Bill's exceptional finds in the sand and water of Boston's area beaches:

- Harley Davidson Signature silver ring (1 oz.)
- 22ct Gold ring with Hindu symbol for good luck
- Two 14ct gold/gemstone ring
- 14ct Gold/diamond ring (X pattern)
- 18ct Gold/1.25ct diamond engagement ring

Critical Success Factors

- Use the library and Internet to become familiar with the history of the area you are planning to detect.

- Study tide charts and storm current in relation to wind direction. These factors combine to create areas that trap coins and jewelry.

- Join a metal detecting club in the area you plan to hunt. Buddy up with a "local" to aid your search for older areas to detect.

- Visit a DPW office or garage. Given the right approach, the people there will share and give you a lot of promising lead.

CHAPTER 11

The Trainer
Chuck Smalley

The Mississippi River has long been a major factor in the growth of our nation. Algonquian speaking First Nation members were the earliest recorded inhabitants living along the Mississippi, followed by French Trappers who migrated from Canada in the early 1700s. The French were credited with establishing the first European settlements in the land now known as Illinois. In the mid-1700s the Mississippi became a critical transportation link for people and goods destined for New Orleans, as well as a gateway to western expansion.

The Davenport–Moline-Rock Island Metropolitan Statistical Area is known as the Quad Cities. The Quad Cities, on the shores of the Mississippi, in northwest Illinois, takes in both Iowa and Illinois Counties.

Chuck Smalley lives just up river from the Quad Cities in the small town of Cordova, population less than 400. Chuck has been a Trainer in Industry for 3M, worked for the Cordova Fire Department (Chief for 20 years), and most recently for Minelabs.

Chuck's commitment to metal detecting started in 1972 with a White's Coin Master IV. His passion to find anything that the soil might contain has taken him to Alaska, Wyoming, and Arizona where he has gold claims, to metal detecting in Iowa, Illinois, Florida, Wisconsin, Missouri, and Colorado.

Very early in his metal detecting career, Chuck and his wife Jill traveled to Keokuk, Iowa, where the Des Moines and Mississippi Rivers meet. The town of Keokuk has long been considered a hub of the Tri-State area comprising Illinois, Missouri and Iowa. The area offered the Smalley's the opportunity to detect an area rich in Civil War history, the birthplace of Mark Twain, and a wealth of riverboat nostalgia.

First stop was at the local Sheriff's office to check in and gain permission to detect on town property. Given a yes, they proceeded to detect in a small park near the Court House. As luck would have it an "old timer" was sitting on a bench overlooking the park. After introductions and explaining why they were there, the gentleman offered a history of the town and where the major meeting areas had been in days gone by. Given several places to choose from Chuck and Jill went in separate directions to cover more of the area. A few hours later they met and compared finds. Chuck had found several Indian Head and Wheat pennies, an 1864 Store penny, a Seated half, and a silver dollar. Jill had found over 60 Indian Head pennies including an 1878. To say the least, they were hooked for life.

Some 40+ years later, Chuck is retired, but busier than ever. He is part owner of Shooters & Prospectors (a firearm and metal detecting shop), and Fire Chief for the Town of Cordova. He travels throughout the United States as a Trainer for Minelabs, specializing in the new CTX 3030.

A small sampling of Chuck's memorable finds:

- 1907 "V" Nickel – earliest find
- Cache of Morgan silver dollars
- 1897 O Barber dime
- 1823 Capped Bust half dollar
- 1840 Dime
- 1908 $5 Gold piece

Critical Success Factors

- "Research where your feet are planted. You do not have to travel hundreds of miles to find objects of value. One of my favorite places to detect is within sight of my house."

- Find the "old timers" in town and talk to them. Even better listen, they love to talk about the days gone by and the changes to the town.

- Clues to the oldest properties in town can be determined by going over old tax records. The house may no longer be there, but the land is and still may have objects of interest.

- Old newspaper files are often on the local library's computer system. Pick a year and look for events held at a fairground or picnic area that are no longer in current use.

- Make a business card to give out to introduce yourself.

- Take the time to fully learn your equipment. Leverage the knowledge of the local retailer, club members, or manufacturer's helpline. Many people new to the hobby lose interest because they don't understand their equipment's basic settings and adjustments.

CHAPTER 12
Stress Reducer
Joan Caldas

Bellmore, New York, is a small hamlet with a population of 16,000, located on Long Island's South Shore. Ideally located a short 45-minute ride on the Long Island Railroad to downtown Manhattan's Penn Station, it offers the best of both worlds. Despite its proximity to New York City's cultural, dining, and sporting attractions, Bellmore offers the tranquility and beauty of a small town.

Joan Caldas calls Bellmore home, and is one of thousands of people commuting into "the city" each day, working in the fast-paced, high-stressed environment of the Financial District. About six years ago, Joan's doctor suggested looking for something that would provide a stress outlet from the demands of her work and raising a family.

She recalls, "One day at a local beach, I saw a few people metal detecting and thought maybe I'll do that when I retire. A visit from my brother, who lives in Florida, changed the timetable for me to start my metal detecting journey." He had purchased a White's DFX 300 as a birthday present for me. "I wanted to make up for all the birthday's I had missed due to business and our military duty." This was all the justification her brother needed for encouraging and supporting her new hobby.

The first time out, Joan found a 14ct diamond tennis bracelet, and a few clad coins (a coin made of silver produced after 1964). The hook was set and she became an enthusiastic participant in a newly found stress-reducing hobby.

The next logical step was joining a local metal detecting club, the Atlantic Treasure Club. "My expectation in joining the Club was to learn more about detecting tips and techniques, places to detect, and listen to stories as told by successful members."

Not only does Joan listen and learn from others, she is a prolific freelance writer sharing her metal detecting experiences through the pages off *Western & Eastern Treasure* and *Lost Treasure* magazines. One of her most recent articles appeared in *Western & Eastern Treasure* magazine's March 2015 edition – "The Summer Shark Tail Tale."

Examples of Joan's detecting successes (specific to coins) and sharing with others:

- *Newsday* July 18, 2014 – Treasure Hunters
- *Western & Eastern Treasure* magazine – October 2014/March 2015
- *Lost Treasure* – July 2014
- Over 100 Wheat pennies
- Three Standing Liberty quarters
- 35 Indian Head pennies
- Four Shield nickels
- 1908 Barber dime
- Several Colonial coins
- Enough clad coins to fund a yearly family dinner

Critical Success Factors

- Anyone who enjoys this hobby will enjoy it more by joining a metal detecting club. Tips and Techniques shared by the members can increase the quality and quantity of your finds.
- Find a way to demonstrate good citizenship as a detectorist. Joan was awarded a plaque in recognition

for her work removing potentially dangerous staples from a Roslyn, Long Island, athletic field.

- Unfilled holes on grass or sand can cause injury and a negative view of our hobby. Make certain that you "do the right thing" in your target recovery and ground repair.

CHAPTER 13
Relic Man
Rudy Reeves

Columbia, South Carolina, population 130,000, is the largest city in South Carolina, as well as the state capital. Rich in southern culture and history, Columbia is a relic hunter's dream.

Rudy Reeves was born in Columbia. He has metal detected the parks, hills, and Civil War battlegrounds for nearly 40 years. Rudy began metal detecting in 1977 as a result of being on the road daily interfacing with customers.

He relates, "One day, while talking with a customer, I was shown several jars full of silver coins that he had found metal detecting. I was so impressed that I went out and purchased a detector of my own. At the time, $300 was a huge sum of money for a newlywed to spend on a hobby. My wife's concern was only temporary as I found a gold ring on my first hunt. I spent my first year focused on coins and jewelry, but was quickly drawn to the challenge of discovering and preserving Civil War relics."

In 1978 Rudy founded and became President of the Palmetto Relic Hunters, a group of detectorist whose primary mission is the recovery of Civil War memorabilia. Columbia is virtually at the center of South Carolina, at the crossroads of interstates 20 and 26. Augusta to the southwest, Charleston to the southeast, Charlotte to the north, and Florence to the east, offers a metal detectorist more opportunities to discover Civil War artifacts than one lifetime could possibly cover.

Rudy has a significant collection of relics recovered over the years, but to his credit has searched out sites for the entire club membership to enjoy. The Club has the opportunity to elect a new President each December, "but you could hear a pin drop when I ask for nominations."

Examples of Rudy's focus and success metal detecting Civil War relics:

- Confederate States clip corner buckle – Tennessee

- Confederate States buckle – Georgia

- Over 60 gold wash military buttons

- Twenty+ Script Eye buttons

- Collection of "carved bullets," whistles, chess pieces, figures

- Two-hundred+ Minié balls

- Hundreds of musket balls

Critical Success Factors

- If you have the sort of job that interfaces with customers on a daily basis, if appropriate, strike up a conversation about metal detecting. This can often lead to permission to hunt on private property.

- Follow the "golden rule." Good southern manners can work anywhere. "Yes, Sir," and "Thank You," go a long way when asking permission to hunt on private property.

- Do your research before ever going out the door to detect. When it is too hot or too cold to metal detect, use that time to go over old street maps, topographical maps, and "how to" relic books. Have a plan, don't just go out and expect miracles.

- Your detector is one of your best friends – learn and listen to it.

CHAPTER 14
Mr. War Button
Robert Underwood

Stoneville, North Carolina, is less than an hour's drive from the cities of Winston-Salem and Greensboro to the south, and less than an hour from Danville, Virginia to the north. This area represents the home metal detecting grounds of Robert Underwood. For the past 35 years he has been detecting on plantations, Colonial home sites, and family-owned properties, yielding an amazing collection of over 2000 flat buttons. Robert's collection of rare Revolutionary War, Civil War, and Indian War buttons is so extensive and historically relevant that museums and historical societies borrow them for exhibitions.

Robert was born in Reidsville, North Carolina, population less than 15,000. Reidsville was most known in the late 1800s as a major processing facility for the American Tobacco Company.

After graduating in 1975 from NC State University (Raleigh), with a BS in Biology, Robert took a job in the Water Resources Department in Eden, North Carolina. One day, on an assignment to spread chemicals to destroy pond algae, he lost his college class ring. A co-worker had a metal detector and offered to find the ring. Fortunately the search was a success and they recovered the ring. Robert was so impressed that he ordered a metal detector kit from Heath Kit, and spent a number of evenings assembling and soldering it at the kitchen table. Thus began a 35-year journey focusing on early war artifacts across five states.

Robert considers himself somewhat of an amateur historian. His persistent digging into library archives, genealogical databases, and topographical surveys, have led to his work with the Madison Historical Properties Commission. Robert's story detailing a cooperative effort between the Commission and members of the Old North

State Detectorist Club is featured in the January, 2014, issue of *America Digger* magazine. The result of their efforts was the validation of the historical origins of a home owned by Daniel Jordan in the 1850s.

Examples of Robert's success in recovering artifacts (specifically buttons):

- Button from a cadet attending the Henderson Male Academy of North Carolina. (Valued at $10,000)

- 1850 Mexican soldier's button

- 17th Century British "nipple" button

- Union Soldier Infantry buttons

- Confederate State of Virginia Staff officer's button

- War of 1812 soldier's button

- U.S. Eagle Artillery "A" cuff button

- 1840 Campaign Button – William Henry Harrison

Critical Success Factors

- A relic hunter's challenge begins in the library and town hall, studying the history of troop movements, encampments, and prisoner of war locations.

- Studying old Stage Coach Routes can be a very productive exercise resulting in finding coins and artifacts relative to the 1700s and 1800s.

- Stage Coach Roads often led to home sites. Look for "out of place" flower beds or older standalone, large trees that may indicate a onetime building location.

- Look for higher ground areas adjacent to a Stage Coach road, as these were often used as campsites to stay away from potentially dangerous high water threats in the spring.

- Stay on a relic site until you feel that all potential areas have been covered. Move away from the obvious main campsite and look for high ridges overlooking the area.

- Join the local historical or archeological societies and demonstrate how cooperation with metal detecting organizations can benefit efforts to discover and preserve our history.

CHAPTER 15
Finance to Fun
John Anderson

Mount Shasta, California, is the home of the Mount Shasta Metal Detecting Club and its President John Anderson. John first came to the area on vacation some 60 years ago with his father, fly fishing for salmon and steelhead trout. "It became a yearly event, something I always looked forward to."

After many years in Real Estate Finance for such companies as GMAC, and Bank of America, John took the opportunity to retire and returned to the Mount Shasta area. He purchased a home on 10 acres of land near the original route of the Central Pacific Railroad. John's land contains over 100 apple trees with origins dating back to the mid-1800s. During that time, the original property owners supplied apples to the stagecoach and rail passengers, as well as tourists.

Today, Mount Shasta has become a resort community given its proximity to the headwaters of the Sacramento River, and the many tributaries feeding it. Nearby Trinity National Recreation Area contains over 250,000 acres of hiking, fishing, and canoeing opportunities. In the early 1800s the area was home to the First Nation Okwanuchu tribe, who hunted and trapped the area's rich waters and abundant forests. The major route through the area at the time was known as the Siskiyou Trail, and was to become the route used by the Central Pacific Railroad in 1887. Gold was discovered in the area in 1850 giving rise to a population boom. Gold is still mined in the area, but on the level of a hobby as opposed to a large commercial operation.

John is now a fixture in the community, and a member/chair of the Mount Shasta Fire Department. When he's not giving his time to the Fire Department, John can be found metal detecting at one of the nearby lakes.

His favorite time of the year to metal detect is in the fall when the lakes are drawn down in preparation for the spring runoff. Campsites and swimming areas have produced an abundance of clad, silver, and even gold coins. Not to be overlooked is the ten acres John owns, which produced a cache of eleven silver V Nickels in 2014.

Examples of John's consistence success:

- $10 gold piece
- Cache of Silver V Nickels
- Over 100 Silver Barber, standing and sitting quarters/ half dollars
- Mop bucket full of clad coins

Critical Success Factors

- Obtain a list of lakes that are planned for "draw down" each year. Contact the Department of Fish & Game to determine the schedule.

- The local historical society can be an excellent source for learning where early settlers may have met, or trails they used in and out of town.

- Abandoned gold mines are an excellent place to look for treasure other than gold.

- Look for fruit orchards that may date back to the early settlers. Often people who harvested the fruit dropped coins, jewelry, or other artifacts.

CHAPTER 16
Genesee
Dave Havens

The Genesee Valley Treasure Seekers was founded in 1990, and has grown each year to its current level of 60 members. Headquartered just outside of Rochester, New York, meetings are held each month in the town of Chili. The Club holds hunts the third Saturday of the month from April through October across western New York State.

Rochester was considered the first boomtown in America, due to the growth of Flour Mills along the Genesee River in the early to mid-1800s. It was known as the Flour City until about 1829 when wheat processing transitioned westward. The city then experienced significant growth in the nursery business and earned the title of Flower City. After the Civil War, Rochester gained fame through the work of George Eastman, John Jacob Bausch, and Henry Lomb. Home of Eastman Kodak, Bausch and Lomb, and later Xerox, Rochester became a thriving center of technology and education. The University of Rochester, and the Rochester Institute of Technology (RIT), are recognized around the world for their excellence. Rochester has been nationally ranked as the best place to raise a family, most livable city, and top ranked public schools.

Dave Havens is an active member and officer of the Genesee Valley Treasure Seekers. Dave is in his 15th year as a metal detectorist searching sites in western New York State, with a proven track record of success. Armed with his Minelab Explorer and Excalibur, he focuses on sites that have a history of producing old coins, but are considered too trashy or have high mineralization. "I tend to find sites that others overlook or pass by on purpose." Persistence is the key to sorting through the challenge of a trashy site, listening for that subtle difference in sound between trash and treasure.

Examples of successful detecting:

- Championship gold baseball ring – returned to owner

- Over 900 Indian Head pennies including an 1877

- 1870 Canadian half dollar – No LCW

- Estimated 50 pounds of Wheat pennies

- Several hundred silver coins dating from 1777 to 1964

Critical Success Factors

- Study aerial photographs and old maps to help narrow down high probability areas. "Don't be shy about asking permission to detect private property."

- Explore areas that have produced quality finds in the past, but are too trashy for most detectorists. These sites are often bypassed but, with persistence and slowing sweep speeds, have the potential to continue to produce.

- Spend the time talking to people who may have local knowledge and are willing to share their recommendations on where to hunt.

- Join in and take part in Club hunts. It is a great place to share information and detect on sites where the Club has permission to hunt, but may not be open to an individual. "It always adds to the excitement when you share the experience with another detectorists."

- Have a positive attitude and combine it with patience. The important thing is to have fun and be persistent.

CHAPTER 17
Michigan
Mark Branton

L ivonia, Michigan, is located East of Lake St. Clair, and northwest of Lake Erie, between the cities of Detroit and Ann Arbor. It has been an area with deep roots in agriculture since the time of the Potawatomi First Nation people. For over 100 years sheep, dairy cattle, vegetables, and grains taken from the area supplied food for cities as far away as Detroit. The Industrial Revolution touched the area in 1948 with the opening of a General Motors Transmission factory, and a Ford Parts Depot. Steady growth from 17,000 residents in 1950, to today's population in excess of 100,000, has made Livonia a thriving community. Livonia's leadership has been dedicated to creating a balance of preserving history through land acquisition, and investing in infrastructure to keep up with the demands of the 21st century.

Founded in 1974 by Al and Doris Temple, the Michigan Treasure Hunters has continued to grow and prosper. "Leave it cleaner than we found it," is the Club's motto, and is taken very seriously by its members.

Mark Branton has been elected President for seven years, overseeing Club activities and the continued practice of good citizenship. Given its location, the areas around Livonia offer the metal detectorist a wide selection of sites to detect. The City of Livonia has acquired and preserved 1,800 acres of parks and open land. In addition to detecting on city property, the area offers forests and beach hunting, as well as acres of agricultural fields. Mark has been detecting the area for over 40 years and, has gathered significant knowledge of where the highest probability sites are found.

Examples of his success:

- 1776 Two Spanish reales

- 1921 Morgan Silver dollar

- 1831 Large cent

- Estimated 100,000 coins (clad and silver)

Critical Success Factors

- Knock on doors of private landowners and create agreements to detect their property. Introducing yourself in a courteous manner, explaining what you do and how you do it, goes a long way towards a yes. Letting the landowner know that you will also pick up trash as well as treasure does score points.

- Local libraries hold a vast amount of knowledge that can be directly applied to determining where to detect. Concentrate on early history and ask to look over the old plate or tax maps showing the location of original parks, schools, and streets.

- The most significant characteristic of a good detectorist is to *listen*.

- Listen to your detector, it is an extension of you and requires absolute focus for optimum results.

CHAPTER 18
Floor Man
Doug Sargent

T
he town of Franklin, New Hampshire, population 9,000, is located just north of Concord, the state capitol, and sits at the confluence of the Pemigewasset and Winnipesauke Rivers, forming the Merrimack River. Doug Sargent has called Franklin home from childhood to adulthood, establishing Doug and Son Flooring in 1968.

Doug explains, "The flooring business has been a key success factor in my 15+ years of metal detecting. Very often the people I meet grant permission to metal detect their property, or provide references to other potential sites."

The flooring business, given its physical demands of stretching, pulling, bending, and lifting is a great conditioner for a long day of metal detecting. Doug belongs to and has served as President, Vice President, and Chairman of the Executive Committee for the Granite State Treasure Hunters for Historic Restoration.

Coins are Doug's preferred detecting challenge, but he has accumulated a substantial collection of rings and jewelry,as well. On the coin front, Doug deposited $1,900 in his granddaughter's college fund in 2013, as a result of several years of recovering clad coins. "Recovering clad coins is something that anyone can be successful at."

Schoolyards, picnic areas, public beaches, fairgrounds, and parking lots at ski areas offer the opportunity for the new or experienced metal detectorists to recover both clad and silver coins.

On the silver coin front, Doug has found several hundred nickels, dimes, quarters, and half dollars that are in the process of being graded and categorized.

Examples of his consistent success:

• Ten gold and diamond rings

- Thirty gold wedding bands
- Ninety silver rings
- Eighty+ silver dimes (1804-1964)
- Thirty+ silver quarters (1873-1964)
- Several pounds of Wheat & Indian Head pennies

Critical Success Factors

- Treating people with courtesy and respect, whether it be in business dealings or people you meet in everyday life, often is rewarded in a sale or permission to detect their property.

- Focus on one or two metal detectors and learn what they are telling you. A subtle tone difference may be the clue to digging treasure or trash.

- **SLOW DOWN!** Racing down a site does not support an overlapping sweep. Take half a step and focus on overlapping each sweep. This technique often results in finding treasures others have missed.

CHAPTER 19
The Hoover Man
Kurt Franz

Kurt is a firefighter in a large metropolitan city. He first became interested in metal detecting as a teenager using a Whites XLT. After graduating from high school Kurt focused on becoming a firefighter and starting a family. For fifteen years the XLT gathered dust in a closet until March, 2014.

As Kurt puts it, "Life happened and I forgot about the hobby."

It only took one afternoon of taking the XLT into the backyard for him to be hooked again on the challenges and rewards of metal detecting. So much so, that he began an exhaustive search for a new detector, as well as finding a metal detecting club to join. In April, 2014, Kurt purchased a new Garrett AT Pro, and joined a local metal detecting club.

As a firefighter Kurt's duties require that he often works a twenty-four hour shift. These extended shifts provide a substantial amount of free time to be with his family, and pursue metal detecting. Blessed with an understanding wife, he has been encouraged to keep the coil to the soil on a regular basis.

The members of the metal detecting club that Kurt joined have nicknamed him "Kurt and his Hoover." The name has been well-earned, as his success in vacuuming up targets of interest is evident. In 2014 Kurt recovered an impressive number of coins;

Examples of his consistent success:

- Almost 200 Indian Head pennies
- Two 1864 "L" on ribbon IHP's
- One 1858 Flying Eagle cent
- One 1852 Trime (silver 3 cent piece)

- Seven Shield nickels
- Seven Seated Liberty dimes (1853 being the oldest)
- Twelve U.S. Large cents, including an 1813 Classic Head, and 1797 Draped Bust
- One 1820 1/4 real
- Five Colonial coins, including a 1694 William & Mary half penny

Coins are Kurt's primary focus, but in the process of identifying high potential detecting sites he has also recovered a substantial collection of flat buttons, a number of Civil War bullets, and an impressive haul of silver and gold rings.

Critical Success Factors

- Combining the manufacturer's metal detecting manual and DVD with a wealth of equipment specific information from YouTube. "There is no shortcut to fully understanding the equipment you have."

- As a firefighter Kurt has an in-depth familiarity of the city. He combines that knowledge with studying historical maps detailing old parks, schools, picnic areas, etc.

- "Dig every jumpy, scratchy, or faint sound. The majority of these may turn out to be junk, but I have often been rewarded with deep silver, a ring, or an artifact."

CHAPTER 20
Sister Act
Blaine and Jan

Blaine

Jan

Blaine and her sister Jan have a long distance metal detecting, and often competitive, relationship. Blaine resides in Texas, and Jan in Colorado. From time to time they do get together for either metal detecting, or participating in 5-10K road races. Both subscribe to the belief that staying in good physical shape has had a positive impact on their metal detecting success. Together, in the past ten years of detecting, they have found over 600 rings. They feel proud of this accomplishment, but have experienced greater satisfaction at having returned 70+ rings to their original owners. Blaine and Jan are believers in the advantages of being a member of a metal detecting club, and both have served their respective clubs at the level of President, Secretary, or Executive Board member.

Given the fact that an ocean is a long way away from where either sister resides required a focus on fresh water lakes as potential ring bearing sites. Monitoring lake levels and reviewing old lake maps overlaid with current Google Earth views have led to the discovery of abandoned parks and beaches. Although the Texas drought of the last few years has created hardships for crops and livestock, it has opened up a substantial amount of lakebed areas. Blaine has put many miles on her car traveling to metal detect lakebeds that have a distant history as a park or gathering area. Blaine and Jan do not limit their metal detecting to Texas or Colorado, but travel to New Hampshire and Maine in the summer months to take advantage of lake- and ocean-detecting there.

In addition to the quantity of rings the Sister Act have found, several examples of the quality of their finds are:

- WW II Veteran's 14ct ring (returned to owner)
- 2ct diamond ring

- 14ct gold/amethyst bracelet
- Bronze coin from the Byzantine Empire

Critical Success Factors

- Be prepared to put in a full day on a selected site. Treating the site as a onetime opportunity forces the detectorist to concentrate on creating a strategic plan of attack.

- Determine the best source of lake level information from State Conservation, Fish & Game, or County Water District websites.

- Visit fresh water lakes to determine where beaches or picnic areas may have been located. Stop by the local gas station or convenience market and ask about the history of the area, and who might be a source of information regarding its history.

- Do not overlook stopping by the town offices and talking with the town clerk or tax collector. They often have knowledge of where the oldest properties are located, and whom to speak with to gain permission to detect on their land.

CHAPTER 21
Dodge City
Terry Adams

No other two words in the English language bring to mind such a vivid image of the Old West as the words Dodge City. First Nations people, scouts, trappers, traders, buffalo hunters, settlers on their way west, cowboys, and an assortment of unsavory characters passed through Dodge City, Kansas. During the 1820's wagons headed for the Santa Fe Trail passed by 24 hours a day, seven days a week.

Fort Dodge opened on the Santa Fe Trail in 1869 to protect the settlers and mail carriers traveling west from the Kiowa and Cheyenne First Nations people. The Atchison, Topeka & Santa Fe railroad came to Dodge City in 1872, creating a monumental boom in population growth. This boom and the lack of law enforcement made it a wide-open town with all the problems that comes with that. This all changed around 1878 as famous gunfighters Bat Masterson, Doc Holiday, and Wyatt Earp rode into town, bringing law and order to the citizens of Dodge. The Long Branch Saloon, and the famous Boot Hill, were the beginning and end of many a desperado. Today, Dodge City celebrates and preserves its rich history while keeping focus on the need to create a modern environment fostering managed growth.

Terry Adams calls Dodge City home, and has been roaming the hills and trails metal detector in hand for the past 40 years. Along with metal detecting and certainly supporting it, is his love of history. Terry has become somewhat of a local historian, reading and studying every book on Dodge City and the surrounding area that he can find. This depth of knowledge of the area has led to his correcting many books and articles with observations and hard evidence as to the exact locations of many historic landmarks.

Over the years Terry has become somewhat of a bloodhound sensing high potential areas to detect. "When I look at any location, objects seem to jump out at me. An old tree by itself, square indentations in the ground where a long gone foundation may have been, and vacant corner lots, all get my attention."

The uses of modern tools, such as the Internet, have added to his "scouting tool bag." Google Earth is one such tool that Terry uses regularly. Combining his knowledge of Dodge City through researching books and maps archived in the library, with hours studying Google Earth mapping views, has resulted in identifying early campsites, trail crossings, and remote foundations.

Terry is the founder of Treasure Hunters of Dodge City, sharing his detecting and research knowledge with club members who request it. The recovery of 300 rings in an area with few if any beaches are a testimony to the effectiveness of his abilities and resourcefulness.

Examples of Terry's success:

- Recovery of 300 gold and silver rings
- A platinum ring with 10 diamonds
- A cache of silver and turquoise rings
- A set of wedding and engagement rings with nine diamonds
- Dozens of class rings found and returned to their original owners

Critical Success Factors

- Always be aware of your surroundings when in or out of your car. Take in the total landscape looking for unusual or out of place objects.

- Use the resources of the Internet before going out to detect. A Google Earth view of a site you are considering to detect will often provide clues as to the best starting point or area on which to concentrate.

- Search out and talk to the elders in a community. They often have local knowledge that does not appear in any history books.

- Search out old maps and books relative to your community. Overlaying Google Earth views on old maps may show features leading to a discovery.

CHAPTER 22
Diablo
Mike Losado

Mike Losado is a native Californian, born and raised in Vallejo, California. The city of Vallejo is just 32 miles northeast of San Francisco. It boasts a population of nearly 120,000, and occupies approximately 50 square miles, 20 of which are water from San Pablo Bay, or Mare Island Strait. The City of Vallejo was named after Mexican General Vallejo. California was annexed to the United States in 1846 following the Bear Flag Revolt with Mexico. The area is also known for a number of seismic faults, the most noteworthy of which are the San Andreas and Hayward faults.

Vallejo serves as home base for Mike's metal detecting forays into sites near the cities of Sacramento, Oakland, San Francisco, Woodland, and Mare Island.

Mike has been metal detecting for the past 33 years. His passion for the hobby has taken him to detect throughout California, as well as Hawaii, and most recently Lake Tahoe, Nevada. He is a member of the Mount Diablo Metal Detecting Club, founded in 1979 by Gary Collier. The founding principle of the Club is "Finding treasure in our surroundings, serving our community, and sharing our wonderful hobby with others."

One of the areas Mike targets is construction sites where sidewalks or road beds are being excavated to make room for new buildings or roadways. Following his instincts and targeting these sites has led to two of his most valued finds: an 1872 $5 gold piece, and a 20 cent piece.

A small sampling of Mike's consistent and impressive success:

- Trade Token – Vallejo White Sulfur Springs – circa 1850

- 1872S – $5 gold piece
- 1875 20 cent piece
- Half dimes, dates ranging from 1833 to 1873
- Shield and V Nickels, dates ranging from 1868 to 1891
- Seated dimes, dates ranging from 1839-O to 1887-S
- Several pounds of pre-1964 silver coins

Critical Success Factors

- Must be willing to dig questionable targets. Patience pays off.

- Visit the department of public works in your area to determine where major construction sites are planned.

- If you pass through an older neighborhood and see sidewalks being torn up, stop and ask permission to detect.

- Seek sites that have been hunted out, and take your time detecting very slowly and listening intently for that inbetween the trash signal.

CHAPTER 23
Beachcomber
Alan Sadwin

*W*ebster's *New World College Dictionary* defines beachcomber as a person who spends time on a beach looking for lost or discarded items, natural specimens, etc., that are useful or interesting. Wantagh, New York, is a mecca for beachcombing. It is also known as the gateway to the famous Jones Beach, and attracts an estimated 6 million visitors a year. Wantagh is also close to a number of beaches that can be of interest to treasure hunters. Atlantic, Long, Lido, and Oak Beaches are all within a short driving distance of the town center.

The earliest recorded inhabitants of the area surrounding what is now Wantagh were the Montauk First Nations tribe. Dutch and English settlers were the first Europeans to settle there, creating a farming community in the mid-1600s. In 1674 The Treaty of Westminster signed by the Dutch, incorporated all of Long Island into the British New York Colony. Following the Revolutionary War, Long Island prospered as a farming and commercial fishing center. Today, farming has a far lesser role than that of tourism. Apart from a number of highly prized beaches, a park system also attracts both visitors and the citizens of Wantagh. Cedar Creek Park, Mill Pond Park, Wantagh Park, and Seaman's Neck Park are examples of government focus on land preservation and public usage.

The oldest metal detecting club in the tri-state area calls Wantagh home. The Atlantic Treasure Club (ATC) celebrates its 41st anniversary in 2015. Alan Sadwin has been a longtime member of the ATC having served as its President, Vice-President, and currently editor of the monthly newsletter.

Alan enjoys and is successful at metal detecting the sandy beaches of Long Island. With 20 years of metal detecting experience behind him, Alan has accumulated a wealth of knowledge pertaining to how to read a body of water, and how best to approach a day of beach hunting. Equipped with a White's TDI and a Minelab Excalibur, Alan feels ready for any soil, water, or weather condition. "Often the best days metal detecting the beach are not the best for sunbathing."

Examples of Alan's year after year success:

- 22ct gold ring

- 10ct gold ring with a channel set stone

- Class ring – returned to owner

- Fossil watch

- 1715 Spanish fleet plate

Critical Success Factors

- Locate where known shipwrecks have occurred near shore and methodically hunt that beach area at low tide or following a storm.

- On the most popular beaches, during the "high traffic" summer months, detect the "blanket line" in the evening after the crowds have left.

- With a little research you may be able to locate the lesser known or now closed beaches to detect. Often these beaches draw an older but potentially more affluent crowd.

- If you have the opportunity to hunt Florida's Treasure Coast, be on the lookout for emeralds in the sand. This is a leading indicator that Spanish Cobs may be present.

- Many people will point to the local library as a source of information relative to early maps. There is no substitute for doing your homework at the library. Bits of information gathered in a day of research will lead to private property that has not been hunted. A courteous approach to a private landowner can result in a "yes," and even more importantly a referral to a friend who also has land.

CHAPTER 24
The Newbie
John Ramoska

All of us who took up the metal detecting hobby had to start somewhere. Those first nervous outings attempting to understand our equipment, where to hunt, and how to retrieve a target were somewhat intimidating. Some good advice from the very start helped native Chicagoan John Ramoska achieve success in his first year of detecting. Equipment was the initial challenge. John's vision was to detect on land and in the water. For water he was advised to purchase a Garrett AT Pro, and for land a Whites MXT Pro. Following that good advice the next suggestion was to find and join an established metal detecting club.

The Midwest Historical Research Society (MHRS) founded in 1968, was an excellent choice, and has proven to be a key to John's out of the gate success. John took it upon himself to search out club members who had the same equipment he had purchased in the hopes of shortening his learning curve. The mentoring that John received from three club members was something he is eternally grateful for.

Chicago is the third largest city in the United States, with a population of nearly 3 million. From its humble beginnings in 1833 with approximately 200 citizens, it has grown to become a center of finance, technology, and shipping. The area has proven to be a metal detectorist heaven with 31 beaches along Lake Michigan, and approximately 50 parks open for public access. North Ave, Fosters, Wyola, 12th Street, and 32nd Street beaches are all on John's hit list.

On the park side John frequents the 1,200-acre Lincoln Park (Civil War Encampment), and the 550-acre Jackson Park. Having a career with the Chicago Department of Transportation (CDOT), has helped John's knowledge of the best beaches to detect, and the highest potential locations within the parks.

Examples of John's successes to date:

- Two finds published in *Garrett's* magazine
- Forty gold and silver rings, including a diamond and platinum wedding ring
- 1853 Indian Head penny
- U.S. Naval uniform button worn in either the Civil War or Spanish-American War
- Several Civil War 3-ring bullets

Critical Success Factors

- Join a Club and seek out a mentor, or mentors, early in your metal detecting career.

- **SLOW DOWN!** One of the most frequent problems people new to the hobby have is going too fast. Being the fastest detectorist is not an effective method of finding the most treasures.

- During your first year dig everything until you get to know the equipment and its ability to separate good targets from junk.

- Do not set unrealistic expectations each time you go into the field. If you set out to profit from this hobby, chances are you will be disappointed. Enjoy the day, your fellow detectorists, and whatever the next beep brings.

CHAPTER 25
Man of Many Hats
Steve Linder

T his is the story of a very interesting individual who clearly fits the "man of many hats" title. Steve Linder's credentials span simultaneous career fields including Insurance Agent/Owner, licensed Auctioneer, licensed Pyrotechnic Operator, Inventor, Microsoft Trainer, and finally, lifelong metal detectorist. His search for artifacts has taken him across nine states: Oklahoma, Tennessee, Missouri, Kentucky, Indiana, West Virginia, Michigan, Georgia, and finally Florida.

In 1974, Steve actually built his first metal detector from scratch. It consisted of a transmitter and receiver, a meter, and a length of plywood. Serving as an all-metal detecting device, it bounced a signal off an object and triggered through the receiver to the meter. As basic as the device sounds, it was a beginning and did function as designed, serving his needs at the time.

Specializing in Civil War artifacts, Steve has traced many of the battles within and across state lines. His approach to determining where to search is worth a second look. Often a battle site serves as a prime area to detect, but may be on property banned for metal detecting by local, state, or the Federal Government. Or, it might be in an area that has been saturated by past detectors. Studying a potential area and determining the routes to and from the battlefield, and in particular areas where solders may have camped and slept, often produces the most relevant finds. Using this method Steve was able isolate a potentially productive area and fine-tune his focus to a specific pathway. This fine-tuning aspect of the search came from taking an old hand-drawn battle map of the area door-to-door and asking for local knowledge. This approach does not always work, but with the right attitude and salesmanship it can be helpful. In this case, local knowledge pinpointed an encampment 400 yards away from the battleground on private lands. After gaining permission to search the property for artifacts, he was able to trace the paths to and from the battle resulting in filling a five-gallon bucket with bullets, buckles, and buttons in a three day period.

Examples of Steve's cross-state adventures searching for Civil War and other research driven property:

- Tennessee – Recovered over 150 military uniform buttons, and filled a five-gallon bucket with dropped and shot bullets of various sizes.

- West Virginia – Collected cannon balls, fuses, buckles, and knife blades.

- Indiana – recovered over 100 coins from the early 1900s

- Pennsylvania – Research led to an old ghost town dating to the Civil War. Recovered a silver buckle, several coins from the 1800s, a Union Soldier's reunion medal dated September 14, 1912, Lakemout Park, and a "Union is Forever" button.

- Florida – Site of an old casino yielded $34 in face value silver coins including nickels, dimes, quarters, and half dollars.

Critical Success Factors

- Make a point of seeking out the elders in a community to ask the question, "What used to be?" The information they have is often not found in the documented history of the town. Visit a senior citizen's center and arrange to give a presentation on metal detecting. All this can lead to some amazing leads.

- Learn how to ask the right questions. Do you remember where the oldest house, park, or school was in town? Can you recall where the first soda fountain was in town? Where did you "hang out" as a teenager? Make a list of open-ended questions that can stimulate a lively conversation.

- Remember the three R's: READ, RESEARCH, and RECOVER. There are no shortcuts to achieving consistent success metal detecting.

- The one thing to keep in mind is that everything still exists somewhere. Be patient and persistent starting with preparation before going to the field. Careful planning on the frontend will produce much more interesting finds on a consistent basis.

CHAPTER 26
The Competitor
Cathy Herrin

Cathy Herrin has lived in Alaska since she was five years old. Cathy is the current Secretary of the Alaska Treasure Seekers Society, while her husband Rod is the President.

The Herrin's make their home in Wasilla, Alaska, population 8,000, according to the 2010 census. Wasilla is about 50 miles north of Anchorage, and boasts having Sarah Palin as its one-time mayor before being elected governor, and later in 2008 John McCain's running mate for the Vice-Presidency of the United States.

Cathy entered the world of metal detecting in 1989 because of a Bounty Hunter metal detector her husband had given her as a birthday present. Her goal during her early years of detected was to just "find something." That something turned out to be hundreds of rings, buckets of clad, and dated silver coins. Relics also became part of the "find something" days with one of the best finds being a hewing broad axe head which was specifically shaped for putting flat sides on timbers.

One of the most unusual requests Cathy has had was when a woman asked her help locating a gold crown tooth. The woman had swallowed the tooth in her sleep and wanted to know if it was still in her "plumbing." Cathy planned to detect Local Park and agreed to meet the woman at that location. Acting somewhat like a TSA agent, Cathy scanned the woman with her detector and verified that the tooth was still in its owner's digestive track.

While Cathy's real detecting passion is coin shooting, she enjoys relic hunting, and competition hunting events. In the past several years she has done very well, having won a number of detectors along with dozens of lesser prizes. "The thrill of competition, the opportunity to measure your skills against others, and the chance to win valuable prizes keeps me focused on trying to improve."

The detectors Cathy and her husband have won or owned are: the original 1989 birthday present Bounty Hunter Quick Draw (still in service); Fisher models 1270, Gold Strike CZ3D, CZ20; Garrett 150, 250, 350; and an AT PRO.

Critical Success Factors

- Fit the detector to the type of detecting you intend to pursue. As an example, competitive events require a fast recovery. For competition Cathy prefers the Fisher 1270 because of its excellent recovery and pinpointing ability.

- If you want to be good at something, spend the hours required to do it. Cathy has put hour after hour into fine-tuning her competitive skillset, including the equipment she uses.

- Use the vast amount of information on the Internet. YouTube is an excellent source of equipment information, other detectorist field experience, and practical how-to tips.

- Join a metal detecting club and leverage the information gained by listening to and watching others detect.

- Find the detector that serves you best and stay with it. Jumping from detector to detector is not the answer, very often it is the person behind the detector fully understanding its capabilities that forms a winning combination.

CHAPTER 27
Merchant Seaman Ivan Salis

J acksonville is the largest city in Florida by population as well as contiguous area. Boasting a population of approximately 850,000, and an area of 875 square miles, Jacksonville offers an attractive climate, culture, and recreational environment for its citizens, as well as metal detectorists. Early ships from Spain, France, and Great Britain passed by Jacksonville before turning east to return to their home ports in Europe. In addition to being on major shipping routes to and from Europe, it is rich in historic battles from the early Indian and French, to the Spanish and English, and then the Civil War.

Ivan Salis lives in Callahan, Florida, just north of Jacksonville. He has swung a detector for over 35 years.

Ivan spent 27 years as a Merchant Seaman, and as a Chief Stewart. He can trace his ancestors, as seamen, back some 300 years. The love of the sea is something that Ivan feels is hardwired into his soul.

After retiring from his career as a Merchant Seaman, he has spent countless hours researching sunken ships and battlegrounds in the Jacksonville area. Research takes on a special meaning when it comes to the depth Ivan takes in tracking down evidence of a shipwreck, or determining exactly where an historic battle may have occurred. Books, maps, storm history, ship's logs, word of mouth passed along by generations of seamen, as well as Civil War pictures, all come into play as he takes on the role of history detective.

Ivan has earned the title of "history dude" given by area school students as a result of his many Civil War presentations. The end result of his research has been the accumulation of a substantial collection of coins and artifacts left behind by travelers, soldiers, and seamen.

Of particular note is the work Ivan has spent determining the locations of the encampments and battlegrounds of the wars that were fought in the Jacksonville area. Clues taken from enlarged photographs to enhance the visual information have often led to historically relevant finds. Belt buckles, bullets, buttons, and war memorabilia from the French, Spanish, English, and Union Solders are all part of his collection.

In 1901, a huge fire took place in Jacksonville that destroyed a large number of homes, hotels, and businesses. By carefully and extensively going over historical maps, and overlaying them on current street maps, Ivan has been able to sort and sift through a wealth of information, resulting in his ability to pin point where some of these landmarks were. Ivan is a pleasure to talk with, and his commitment to finding the "devil in the detail" of historical documents is informative and refreshing.

A sampling of Ivan's finds to date:

- Discovered a Civil War encampment occupied by Major Samuel Sherer

- Extensive collection/inventory of artifacts from the Civil War

- Seminole War era flintlock – lock works

- 1866 Dime, 1 of 8,000 minted

Critical Success Factors

- Listen to what your detector is saying before looking at the display. Learning the tone differences can result in fewer trash digs. Combining the sound and then the display technique may result in improved finds.

- Understanding that the ground can only "take in" as much signal as the soil condition (mineral content) will allow. Putting out as much signal as the ground can absorb is called "grounding." Trying to "push" more signal than the ground can absorb is often counterproductive.

- When using a detector on a beach with excessive mineralization, back off on sensitivity until it stabilizes.

- In depth research is often the key to better results. Treating research with a detective's attitude can be very rewarding.

CHAPTER 28
Fisherman
Frank Juarez

Frank Juarez of Davenport, Iowa, has only two hobbies, but they take very much the same skillset. Fishing for Crappie and Walleye Pike is one passion, and the other is metal detecting. Having patience, locating where the fish are, and having the right equipment to do the job can be directly related to metal detecting. Frank began his metal detecting career some 20 years ago starting with a White's Coin Master. His fishing career started many years before metal detecting, but the skills honed in nearby lakes and streams were readily applied. Finding where to have the highest probability of success on the water required reading books and maps about local lakes, stocking information, and state fisheries' publications.

Frank's metal detecting success can be attributed to spending hours in the local library and on the Internet piecing together bits of information and clues as to where the best places are to metal detect. As Frank puts it, "The Internet has changed everything. I save countless hours avoiding metal detecting non-productive areas by taking very early town maps showing homes, parks, and farmlands, and then overlaying them on a Google Earth view."

One example of his out-of-the-box thinking when it comes to locating new ground to detect is to review the lost and found sections of old newspapers. Quite often a location is given where the person may have lost an item, providing a clue as to where a now forgotten park, church, or athletic field had been located. Taking this information and then applying Internet available tools has helped him put together his targeted area list each year before going into the field.

Frank does not have to travel far from his home in Davenport to find places to detect. The Quad Cities area, that Davenport is part of, has an extensive public parks system to choose from.

Frank is also a member of the not-for-profit Gateway Development Group, that rescues old homes condemned by the city to be torn down. The group is given a set amount of time by the city to salvage anything of value from these homes and resell those items to support reinvesting in homes that can be restored. In the course of assisting in these recover and restore activities, Frank does have the opportunity to detect some of the older properties in the area, which has added to his personal collection of interesting finds. Many of the items found are given to landowners, or shared with the Rock Island County Historical Society, of which he is a member.

Some examples of his finds recovered in the past year:

- Gold-plated Civil War timepiece

- Round plate that would go on a horse's harness with an 1880 date and inscription: George Lauv & Son Tanners of Harness Leathers

- Set of sleigh bells with an inscribed 1850 date

- Toy cap gun and toy derringer from the 1930's

- Over fifty silver coins dating from 1889 to 1964

Critical Success Factors

- Joining a community improvement organization and/or local Historical Society can spread the good that metal detectorist can provide while increasing personal satisfaction.

- Research and support tools offered by the Internet are one of your best friends when it comes to locating interesting areas to detect. Too many people are intimidated by the Internet, or just plain lazy when it comes to research.

- The experience of metal detecting or research is much more enjoyable when shared with a friend or a metal detecting club.

- Not properly filling the holes dug in the process of recovering a target is the number one reason private and public property owners give when areas become closed to detecting. *FILL YOUR HOLES PROPERLY!*

CHAPTER 29
Answer Man
Moe DiPinto

One of the most respected individuals in the metal detecting community is Moe DiPinto, the *Answer Man.* Moe has worked for the past eight years for one of the major providers of metal detectors and accessories as their leading product support specialist.

He began metal detecting in 1989 with a White's Coinmaster. At that time Moe worked as a contactor in central Massachusetts, traveling daily to urban and rural worksites. Very often he would come across site excavations or older home renovations that led to metal detecting opportunities.

He focused his metal detecting on coins recovered from old homesites and farmland. Moe successfully found a substantial number of old copper and silver coins. He then turned towards the ocean and began detecting for jewelry. Not too many people would wade waist deep in the ocean, particularly during the winter months, when he began focusing on metal detecting in the ocean. More than once he was approached by a game warden suspecting him of collecting clams out of season.

The most interesting story Moe tells involved a day wading in the ocean. "I was suddenly surrounded by several police with their guns drawn. It seems that someone had called the police reporting that they saw someone disposing of a body. It took some time and convincing the police that I was only metal detecting." Although the incident did provide some anxious moments, it did not dampen his desire and commitment to continue metal detect the beaches of Massachusetts, Rhode Island, and New Hampshire.

The daily requirement of his current job is to talk to people from around the world, answering technical questions, or optimizing a program specific for a detector. Moe never tires of the daily immersion in metal detector phone calls, and looks forward to weekends when he can head for a beach to detect. "One of the perks of the job is that I have the opportunity to field test the new detectors our suppliers send us. This gives me the ability to not only have fun using the detectors, but provide real field experience answers to the people who call." This daily contact with the metal detectorists audience has often brought with it invitations to detect highly productive private properties.

While "having fun" Moe has recovered some very interesting and valuable finds:

- Nazi U-boat commander's ring

- Many gold and diamond rings

- Antique 18ct white gold wedding ring

- 24ct gold engagement ring

- 1727 Spanish real

- Collection of Large Cents 1803-1850

Critical Success Factors

- Start each metal detecting adventure in "all metal" mode. This will provide clues as to what the age of the property is by the type of trash found.

- Understand the relationship between ground balance and swing speed. If the iron content of the soil is high, slow down your swing speed to compensate. If the area is known to be of historical significance, it is important to go over the ground in three passes. north-south, east-west, and diagonally. This method will help overcome any iron masking due to soil composition.

- Always be aware of your surroundings in terms of metal detecting opportunities. Carry a metal detector in your car to take advantage of spontaneous opportunities.

- Before planning a trip to the ocean to detect during the winter months, before or after a storm, consult the National Oceanic and Atmospheric Administration (NOAA) website (www.noaa.gov), to determine the predicted tide times and wave characteristics. After some trial and error you'll be able to use this information to determine the most favorable conditions in which to detect.

CHAPTER 30
Ray the Barber
Ray Grypp

W hat do successful bartenders, psychiatrists, and barbers have in common? The answer is very simple: they are experts at the art of communication. Their success depends on stimulating interesting and informative discussions. That ability has been the key to metal detecting success for Ray Grypp of Illinois.

Ray was a successful barber for over 40 years and leveraged his occupation into his hobby. At one time or another, every customer who entered his place of business was introduced to the subject of metal detecting. These conversations often led to permission to hunt on private lands, or produced a lead that identified public property that once was the site of a park, school, or fairground. Customers spread the word of Ray's interest in metal detecting, leading to even more opportunities to detect on private land.

To fine-tune and sort through all of the opportunities to detect on private or public land, Ray spends time on in-depth research. Being somewhat of a history buff, he has acquired an impressive collection of history books specific to rural Illinois communities. Biographies of local residents, old plat maps, town histories, and books detailing civil war activities combined with "barber shop referrals" have resulted in a valuable coin collection.

Ray has metal detected in Alaska, Florida, Iowa, California, Nebraska, Kansas, Missouri, and Illinois. Although his main focus is old home sites, ghost towns, and fairgrounds in Illinois and Iowa, the lure of gold in Alaska, and jewelry in the waters of Florida, have tempted him on more than one occasion.

"At the end of the day, it's the old and forgotten farm fields and homesites that keep my interest. Give me an old cellar hole and a sandwich and I'm good for the day."

His most noteworthy success at metal detecting has earned him the nickname "Ray The Barber." The name has little to do with his expertise as a barber, but from finding nearly 400 Barber coins – dimes, quarters, and half dollars.

Examples of the quality of coins in Ray's collection:

- Estimated 400 Barber coins (many with prized dates)
- 1877 Indian Head penny
- 1916D Mercury dime
- 1909 $5 Gold piece
- 1875 Twenty cent piece

Critical Success Factors

- Talk to people, introduce yourself, and tell them about your hobby. A brief conversation can lead to a successful day detecting.

- There are no shortcuts to consistently successful metal detecting. Spending as much time researching your next hunt site as actually hunting will result in a much higher probability of success.

- A good lead, validated by research, combined with persistence, has led to my success and will work for anyone serious about metal detecting.

CHAPTER 31
Plymouthian
Kent Blethen

I first met Kent in 2014 at an exhibition sponsored by the Silver City Treasure Seekers of Massachusetts. Kent had the first booth close to the entrance. What drew my attention was that he had decorated a large aquarium with many of the rings, coins, and jewelry he had recovered from beaches in southern Massachusetts and northern Rhode Island. In addition to the aquarium display he had several trays full of silver, gold, and diamond rings. In the past three years alone Kent has detected and recovered over 200 rings. There is a friendly competition among his friends defined by who recovers the most diamonds in a given year. All diamonds count from diamond chips to stand alone stones. In 2014 Kent was the winner with 93 diamonds!

The winter storms that often plague the northeast do not keep him from metal detecting the beaches. According to Kent, "A storm by itself does not guarantee that you will find something of value. I focus my efforts on looking for cuts, specifically washed out areas that may reveal hidden rocks." As the tide recedes following a storm, those areas become evident and bear stopping and detecting. "During the summer months I tend to follow the crowds, waiting until late afternoon or evening to detect. Winter has become my favorite time to detect as the crowds are gone and only we diehards are willing to brave the cold and wind."

Another source of detecting success comes from Kent being an avid deer hunter. In addition to scouting for deer, he is ever on the alert for remote cellar holes that might have the promise of artifacts or old coins. Planning ahead to the 2016 Club Exhibition, coins and artifacts found by his targeting old cellar holes will be on display, as well as a much larger aquarium filled with beach bounty from the last two years.

Examples of Kent's detecting success:

- Gold Rolex watch
- A 1.25ct Diamond ring lost by its owner in 1998. Kent found and returned it in 2013.
- WWI 12th Division 35 machine gun battalion gold ring
- 1919 Teddy Roosevelt pipe
- 115 Gold rings
- 125 Silver rings

Critical Success Factors

- Do not waist time detecting a beach without focusing on a specific area. Drive from beach to beach, if necessary, until new cut areas appear, or where you have observed cut areas in the past.

- A waterproof detector is a better choice in the winter as the opportunity to drop a machine into the surf, due to cold hands, is an expensive lesson to learn.

- Experience dictates to dig every target as a valuable target that might be masked by iron.

- Find a detector that you have confidence in and do not put it down or purchase another until you have fully learned its capabilities. Build upon detector knowledge as opposed to chasing technology. Unless you are willing to spend the time fully learning the capabilities of your detector, new technology will not increase your chances of success.

CHAPTER 32
Club Hunt Master

One of the more challenging positions in any Metal Detecting Club is that of Hunt Master. He or she is responsible for:

- Finding sites large enough to accommodate all the members signed up to hunt (including parking)

- Negotiating "Private Land" use fees with the property owner

- Obtaining the necessary permits required for municipal properties

- Providing proof of liability insurance (should it be required)

- Assuring that restroom facilities are available for the hunt

- Communicating details of the hunt site and hours to the membership

- Patrolling the site during the hunt to assure that the members are safe and within the approved boundaries

- Patrolling the hunt site after the hunt to ensure that best digging practices have been followed

In the course of interviewing detectorist for this book, the subject of arranging a Club Hunt was often discussed. The most challenging aspect being locating property that has a high potential for finding old coins, artifacts, and jewelry.

Here are some of the "out of the box" thinking that was shared related to finding areas for a group to detect;

- Research all farms built prior to 1900 that are for sale

- Research all homes built prior to 1900 that are for sale
- Make a list of the oldest apple or fruit orchards
- Make a list of all closed drive-in theaters
- Make a list of all fresh and saltwater beaches
- Make a list of all scouting and private youth camps
- Making a list of all present and past fairground sites
- Make a list of all campgrounds, both public and private
- Make a list of all ponds and lakes drawn down for winter runoff

The research is best done in the offseason when properties are not as active with summer activities such as youth camps, or farms (planting and harvesting will prevent you getting permission to metal detect). In all cases, an initial sort of the list based on property size and age helps to establish a target list.

One person interviewed described a "research day" where members of the Club meet at the local library, dive into the historical archives, and come up with a list of potential properties. Personal visits with property owners, private or municipal, is an absolute requirement to gain permission for the hunt. Informing the property owner of the Club's history, mission statement, and ethical practices goes a long way towards gaining a yes. One extremely important gesture is to inform the property owner that the participating members will remove all trash found in the process of recovering a target. Filling a contractor's bag full of paper, cans, bottles, or general trash is a win for both the Club and the landowner.

GOOD HUNTING!

Author Biography

    T. D. Bunce (Tom) lives in Londonderry, New Hampshire, with his wife Karen, and Golden Retriever River. Tom is an active member of the Granite State Treasure Hunters for Historic Preservation, and has served as an Officer, and a member of the Executive Committee.

Printed in Great Britain
by Amazon.co.uk, Ltd.,
Marston Gate.